EZRA LADERMAN

VIOLIN DUETS

ED 4203
First Printing: April 2005

ISBN 0-634-09621-4

G. SCHIRMER, *Inc.*

DISTRIBUTED BY

HAL•LEONARD®
CORPORATION
7777 W. BLUEMOUND RD. P.O. BOX 13819 MILWAUKEE, WI 53213

for Aimlee
VIOLIN DUETS
I

Ezra Laderman

Copyright © 2000 by G.Schirmer, Inc. (ASCAP), New York, NY
International copyright secured. All Rights Reserved.
Warning: Unauthorized reproduction of this publication is
prohibited by Federal law and subject to criminal prosecution.

II

III

Allegro molto

IV

Moderato

V

Allegro con brio (scherzando)

VI

VII

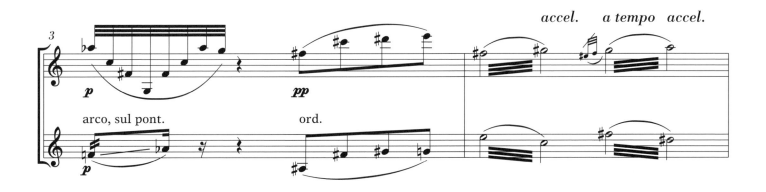

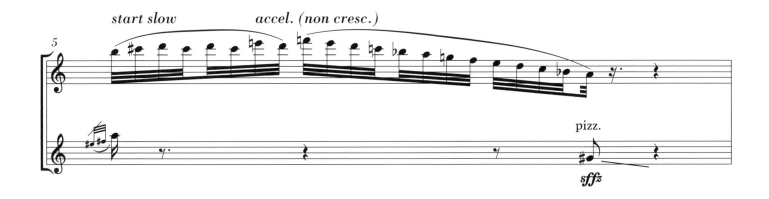

VIII

Swinging (moderato)

*: This duet is to be played twice, with violinists switching parts upon the repeat.

IX

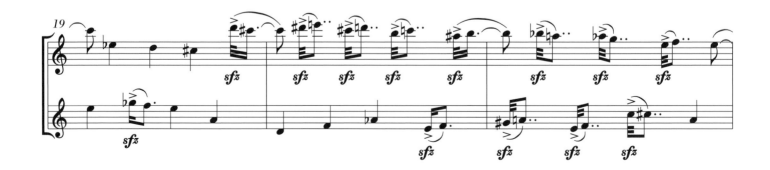

X

Graceful and playful, yet wistful

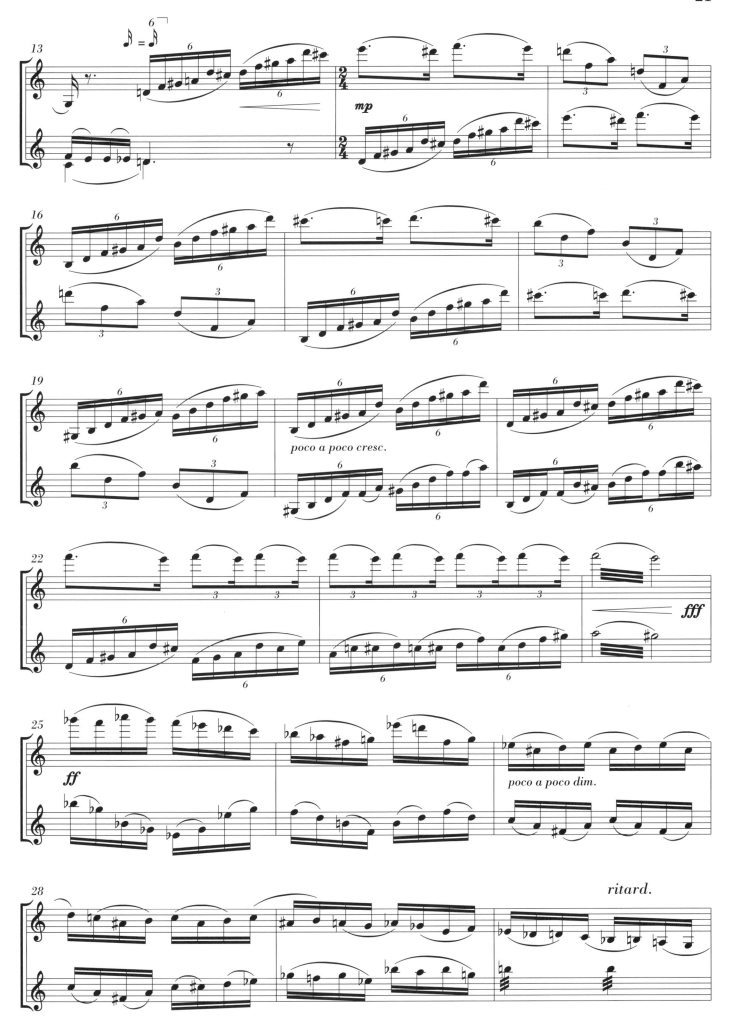

Woods Hole
July 29,1998

G. SCHIRMER, Inc.

DISTRIBUTED BY

HAL•LEONARD®